*the* CONCERT PERFORMER SERIES



# Beethoven

## *Moonlight Sonata*

Exclusively Distributed By
HAL•LEONARD®

# Moonlight Sonata

Ludwig van Beethoven

una corda
marcato, ma sempre p
pp
cresc.
dimin.
p una corda
pp
il basso sempre
p
pp

pp
p
cresc.
dim.
espress.
p
mf
dim.
una corda
poco riten.
a tempo
pp
grave
più marcato del principio
p
Ped.
p
un poco
cresc.
più cresc.
p subito
Ped.

piu p
pp
Ped.
Ped.
Ped.
Ped.
sempre legatissimo
una corda
dimin.
Ped.
slentando
pp
ppp

Project editor: Peter Pickow



Order No. AM948662
International Standard Book Number: 0.8256.1 734.0